Nonprofit Resources

A Companion to Nonprofit Governance

Editor
Victor Futter

American Society of
Corporate Secretaries

Section of Business Law
American Bar Association

Library of Congress Cataloging-in-Publication Data

Nonprofit resources : a companion to Nonprofit governance / editor,
Victor Futter.
    p. cm.
Includes bibliographical references.
  ISBN 1-59031-042-X (pbk.)
  1. Nonprofit organizations—Law and legislation—United
States—Bibliography. 2. Nonprofit organizations—Management—Bibliography.
I. Futter, Victor, - II.
Nonprofit governance and management.

  KF1388.A1 N66 2002
  658'.048—dc21   2002004236

Discounts are available for books ordered in bulk. Special consideration is given to state bars, CLE programs, and other bar-related organizations. Inquire at Publications Planning & Marketing, American Bar Association, 750 North Lake Shore Drive, Chicago, Illinois 60611

07 06 05 04 03 02   6 5 4 3 2 1

Contents

Introductory Note

Nonprofit Resources is a compilation of helpful references on a range of topics in the nonprofit field rather than a comprehensive guide or bibliography. The latter would be a compendium of enormous size and its very size would reduce its usefulness. But winnowing down such references begs the question of how the selections were made. We have tried to pick a variety of references that we think will be useful and provide a running start on any given topic. We hope our readers will be able to avoid the necessity of painstakingly pursuing a digest or index of periodicals, cases or statutes.

We have sought to distinguish this book from other bibliographies by arranging the references topically rather than alphabetically. References beneath each topic are divided into four categories: bibliography (printed references such as books, journal articles, and brochures); case law; statutory and other authority; and Internet sites. In addition, at the end, under "Additional Internet Resources," we have pooled all of web sites listed under the various topics, as well as added a number of prominent resources available through the Internet. We believe that this book will prove to be a valuable supplement to *Nonprofit Governance and Management*.

For ease of reference, we have included most of the references listed at the end of each chapter of *Nonprofit Governance and Management* and have supplemented these with additional resources.

We are indebted to Lizabeth A. Moody, Lynn A. Howell, Nina L. Mings and Stetson University School of Law for their help in preparing this Sourcebook, as well as to Barbara Bryan of the New York

Regional Association of Grantmakers for her helpful comments. We would also like to thank Erin MacMillan of the American Bar Association, Savvas Foukas of Hughes Hubbard and Reed, and Lisa A. Runquist for assisting in the copyediting of the text. And, above all, we owe a debt of gratitude to Judith F. Anspach, Director of the Law Library at Hofstra University School of Law, for her considerable help in endeavoring to correct errant citations.

We welcome the suggestions of our readers concerning items which should be added to, deleted from or recategorized in future editions.

VICTOR FUTTER
Editor-in-Chief

Resources by Topic

Resources by Topic

Accountability

Bibliography

James C. Collins & Jerry I. Porras, Built to Last: Successful Habits of Visionary Companies (1997).

Fisher Howe, *Nonprofit Accountability,* Nonprofit World, November/December 2000.

William Meehan & Les Silverman, *For Charities, Performance Is the New Ethic,* Leader to Leader, Fall 2001, at 13.

Gary J. Stern, et al., The Drucker Foundation Self-Assessment Tool: Participant Workbook (2d rev. ed., Jossey-Bass 1998).

Gary J. Stern, et al., The Drucker Foundation Self-Assessment Tool: Process Guide (2d rev. ed., Jossey-Bass 1998).

Accounting

Bibliography

Accounting Irregularities and Financial Fraud (Michael R. Young ed., 2001).

3

Coopers & Lybrand, Financial Reporting and Contributions: A Decision Making Guide to FASB Nos. 116 and 117 (1995).

Coopers & Lybrand, Financial Reporting and Contributions: Guidance for Implementation of FASB Nos. 116 and 117 (1994).

Antitrust

Bibliography

Peter James Kolovos, Notes, *Antitrust Law & Nonprofit Organizations: The Law School Accredition Case*, 71 N.Y.U. L. Rev. 689 (1996).

Srikanth Srinvasan, Notes to The Board of Trustees of Leland Stanford, Jr. University, College Financial Aid and Antitrust: Applying the Sherman Act to Collaborative Nonprofit Activity, (1994).

Case Law

American Soc'y of Mech. Eng'r, Inc. v. Hydrolevel Corp., 456 U.S. 556 (1982).

United States v. Rockford Mem'l Corp., 898 F.2d 1278, (7th Cir. 1990), *cert. denied*, 498 U.S. 920.

Assessment

Bibliography

Anthony J. Gambino & Thomas J. Reardon, Financial Planning and Evaluation for the Nonprofit Organization (1981).

Harry P. Hatry, Elaine Morley, & Elisa Vinson, Outcome Measurement in Nonprofit Organizations: Current Practices and Recommendations (Independent Sector 2001).

Thomas P. Holland & Myra Blackmon, Measuring Board Effectiveness (National Center for Nonprofit Boards 2000).

Rob Reider, Improving the Economy, Efficiency, and Effectiveness of Not-for-Profits: Conducting Operational Reviews (John Wiley & Sons 2001).

Internet Sites

The Peter F. Drucker Foundation for Nonprofit Management, Drucker Foundation Self-Assessment Tool (The Peter F. Drucker Foundation & Jossey-Bass 1993), *available at* <http://www.pfdf.org>.

Statutory and Other Authority

Revised Model Nonprofit Corp. Act §§ 1.70, 8.10 (1988).
Ala. Code § 13A-9-76 (1975).
Conn. Gen. Stat. § 21a-1901 (1958).
D.C. Code Ann. § 2-712 (1981).
Ill. Comp. Stat. (1993).
Ind. Code § 23-7-8-8 (1976).
Iowa Code § 504 A. 53 (1946).
Mass. Gen. Laws ch. 180, § (1958).
Nev. Rev. Stat. § 82.536 (1957).
N.J. Stat. Ann. § 45: 17A–33 1937.
N.M. Stat. Ann. § 57-22-9 (1978).
N.Y. Not-for-Profit Corp. Law § 112 (McKinney 1997).
Or. Rev. Stat. § 128.710 (1953).
S.D. Codified Laws § 47-26-16 (1967).
Wash. Rev. Code §§ 1909.277, 19.09.410 (2001).
Wis. Stat. § 440.475 (2000).

Attorney General

Bibliography

David Villar Patton, *The Queen, The Attorney General, and the Modern Charitable Fiduciary: A Historical Perspective on Charitable Enforcement and Reform*, U. Fla. J.L. & Pub. Poly 131 (Spring 2000).

Internet Sites

National Association of Attorneys General (contains information about the offices around the country, including addresses and phone numbers), <http://www.naag.org>.

New York State Attorney General (contains a subdivision about the Charities Bureau and the New York charities laws), <http://www.oag.state.ny.us>.

Charity

Bibliography

BRUCE R. HOPKINS, THE LAW OF TAX-EXEMPT ORGANIZATIONS, 7TH EDITION ch. 6 (John Wiley & Sons 1998).

Case Law

Child v. U.S., 540 F.2d 597 (2d Cir. 1976), *cert. denied*, 429 U.S. 1092 (1977).

DeCosta v. DePaz, 2 Swans 487 (Chancery, 1754).

Eastern Kentucky Welfare Rights Org. v. Simon, 506 F.2d 1278 (D.C. Cir. 1974); *vacated and rem'd on other grounds*, 426 U.S. 26 (1976).

Jackson v. Phillips, 96 Mass. 539 (1867).

Plumstead Theatre Soc'y, Inc. v. Commissioner, 74 T.C. 1324 (1980).

Re Shaw (deceased). *Public Trustee v. Day and Others*, 1957 1 W.L.R. 729 (Ch.).

Thomason v. Commissioner, 2 T.C. 441 (1943).

Trustees of Dartmouth Coll. vs. Woodward, 17 U.S. (4 Wheat.) 518 (1819).

Trustees of the Philadelphia Baptist Assoc., et al. vs. Hart's Ex'r, 17 U.S. (4 Wheat) 1 (1819).

United States Cancer Council, Inc. v. Commissioner, 165 F.3d 1173 (7th Cir. 1999).

Vidal vs. Girard, 43 U.S. (2 How.) 127 (1844).

Statutory and Other Authority

I.R.C. § 501(c)(3)

Treas. Reg. § 1.170A-4A(b)(2)(ii)(D) (as amended in 1984).

Treas. Reg. § 1.170A-4A(b)(2)(ii)(E) (as amended in 1984).
Treas. Reg. § 1.501(c)(3)-1(d)(2) (as amended in 1990).
Rev. Rul. 69-545, 1969-2 C.B. 117 (1969).
Rev. Rul. 79-17, 1979-1 C.B.193 (1979).
Tax Analysis Document Number: Doc. 2001–2001
Tax Analysis Document Number: Doc. 2001–28182
Tax Analysis Document Number: Doc. 2001–28892
Tax Analysis Document Number: Doc. 2001–28893
Tax Analysis Document Number: Doc. 2001–29249 (20 Nov. 2001).
Tax Analysis Electronic Citation: 2001 TNT 227-2 (20 Nov. 2001).
Tax Analysis Document Number: Doc. 2001–28414
Tax Analysis Document Number: Doc. 2001–29071
The Statute of Elizabeth (the Statute of Uses), 43 Eliz. I c.4 (1601).

Clubs

Bibliography

NATIONAL CLUB ASSOCIATION, FEDERAL TAX TREATMENT OF PRIVATE
  CLUBS (Club Director Reference Series 1993).
Regina E. Herzlinger, *Effective Oversight: A Guide for Nonprofit
  Directors*, HARV. BUS. REV., July-Aug. 1994, at 52.
Fred L. Somers, Jr., *In Club Wars, Privacy and Choice Battle Freedom
  From Discrimination*, BUS. L. TODAY, Nov.-Dec. 1994, at 26.
Fred L. Somers, Jr., *Pivot or Perish*, CLUB DIRECTOR, April 1996, at 4.
Fred L. Somers, Jr., *Prolegomenon to a Right of Private Association*,
  PERSPECTIVE, June 1988, at 22 (National Club Association's maga-
  zine before its current incarnation as CLUB DIRECTOR).
Fred L. Somers, Jr., *Protecting against Public Accommodation
  Legislation*, CLUB DIRECTOR, Sept. 1989, at 9.

Case Law

Board of Directors v. Rotary Club, 481 U.S. 537 (1987).
Borne v. Haverhill Golf Club, Civil Action No. 96-6511-C, Suffolk
  Superior Court (Mass. 1999), appeal pending.
Boy Scouts of America v. James Dale, 530 U.S. 640 (2000).

EEOC v. Chicago Club, 86 F.3d 1423 (7th Cir.1996).
Louisiana Debating & Literary Assoc. v. City of New Orleans, 42 F.3d 1483 (5th Cir. 1995).
N.Y. State Club Assoc. v. City of New York, 487 U.S. 1 (1987).
Roberts v. U.S. Jaycees, 468 U.S. 609 (1984).

Statutory and Other Authority

I.R.C. § 501(c)(7).
N. C. GEN. STAT. § 55A 16-02 (1999).
TENN. CODE ANN. § 48-58-601(c) (1956).
W. Va. S.B. 509 (2002).

Codes of Conduct

See Ethics.

Commerce Clause and Fund Raising

Case Law

American Charities for Reasonable Fundraising Regulation, Inc. v. Pinellas County, 32 F. Supp. 2d 1308 (M.D. Fla. 1998), *aff'd in part, vacated and rem'd in part*, 221 F.3d 1211(11th Cir. 2000).

Compensation

Bibliography

BOARDSOURCE, CHIEF EXECUTIVE COMPENSATION: A GUIDE FOR NONPROFIT BOARDS (BoardSource 1999).
JOSE PIERSON & JOSHUA MINTZ, ASSESSMENT OF THE CHIEF EXECUTIVE (BoardSource 2001).
The PM (Philanthropy Monthly) Annotated Investigative Report on United Way of Americas, THE PHILANTHROPY MONTHLY, Dec. 1991.

Board of Regents of the University of the State of New York, *Report* (1997) in *The Committee to Save Adelphi et al.* against *Peter Diamandopoulos et al.* This Report and the actions therein set forth was affirmed by the Appellate Division of the Supreme Court, *Adelphi University v. Board of Regents of the State of New York, et al.* 229 A.D. 2d 36, 652 N.Y.S. 2d 837 (1997).

Statutory and Other Authority

REVISED MODEL NONPROFIT CORP. ACT §§ 1.70, 8.10 (1988).
ILL. COMP. STAT. (1993).
IND. CODE § 23-7-8-8 (1976).
IOWA CODE § 504 A. 53 (1946).
MASS. GEN. LAWS ch. 180, § (1958).
NEV. REV. STAT. § 82.536 (1957)
N.J. STAT. ANN. § 45: 17A-33 (1937).
N.M. STAT. ANN. § 57-22-9 (1978).
OR. REV. STAT. § 128.710 (1999).
S.D. CODIFIED LAWS § 47-26-16 (1967).
WASH. REV. CODE §§ 1909.277, 19.09.410 (2001).
WIS. STAT. § 440.475 (2000).

Conflicts of Interest

Bibliography

Deborah A. DeMott, *Self-Dealing Transactions in Nonprofit Corporations*, 59 BROOK. L. REV. 131 (1993).
DANIEL L. KURTZ, MANAGING CONFLICTS OF INTEREST: PRACTICAL GUIDELINES FOR NONPROFIT BOARDS (BoardSource 2001).

Corporate Sponsorships

Bibliography

Elizabeth M. Roberts, Note, *Presented to You by...: Corporate Sponsorship and the Unrelated Business Income*, 17 VA. TAX REV. 399 (1997).

La Verne Woods, *Brought to You by the IRS: Proposed Regs on Corporate Sponsorship*, 29 EXEMPT ORG. TAX REV. 425 (2000).

Cy Pres—Power to Vary

Bibliography

Roger G. Sisson, *Relaxing the Dead Hand's Grip: Charitable Efficiency and the Doctrine of Cy Pres*, 74 VA. L. REV. 635 (April 1988).

Grant Williams, *Lawsuit in New York Could Affect Earmarked Funds at 500 Community Foundations*, CHRON. PHILANTHROPY, April 20, 2000, at 26.

Case Law

Alco Gravure, Inc. v. Knapp Found., 479 N.E.2d 752 (N.Y. 1985).

Application of Community Serv. Soc'y of N.Y., 713 N.Y.S.2d 712 (App. Div. 2000).

In re Los Angeles County Pioneer Soc'y, 257 P.2d 1 (Cal. 1953).

In re Matter of Multiple Sclerosis Serv. Org of N.Y., 496 N.E.2d 861 (N.Y. 1986).

Statutory and Other Authority

Treas. Reg. § 1.170A-9(e)(11)(v)(B).

Directors

Bibliography

AMERICAN SOCIETY OF CORPORATE SECRETARIES, DIRECTOR: SELECTION, ORIENTATION, COMPENSATION, EVALUATION AND TERMINATION (1998).

AMERICAN SOCIETY OF CORPORATE SECRETARIES, LOGISTICAL ARRANGEMENTS FOR BOARD MEETINGS (1999).

AMERICAN SOCIETY OF CORPORATE SECRETARIES, MEETINGS OF THE BOARD OF DIRECTORS AND ITS COMMITTEES: A GUIDEBOOK (1985).

AMERICAN SOCIETY OF CORPORATE SECRETARIES, REVIEW OF BOARD PRACTICES BY BOARD OF DIRECTORS (1997).

Bishop Estate Closing Agreement, 27 EXEMPT ORG. TAX REV. 174, 174–81 (2000).

P.K. CHEW, DIRECTOR'S AND OFFICE'S LIABILITY (Practicing Law Institute 1999).

COMMITTEE ON CORPORATE LAWS, CORPORATE DIRECTOR'S GUIDEBOOK, THIRD EDITION (American Bar Association 1994).

Victor Futter, *Advice to the Lovelorn or What Every Director from the For-Profit World Should Know About Nonprofit Organizations*, 69 ANNUAL SURVEY OF BANKRUPTCY LAW, 1999–2000 EDITION (West Group 1999).

GUIDEBOOK FOR DIRECTORS OF NONPROFIT CORPORATIONS (George W. Overton & Jeannie Carmedelle Frey eds., American Bar Association 2nd ed. 2002).

FISHER HOWE, WELCOME TO THE BOARD: YOUR GUIDE TO EFFECTIVE PARTICIPATION (Jossey-Bass 1995).

RICHARD T. INGRAM, TEN BASIC RESPONSIBILITIES OF NONPROFIT BOARDS (National Center for Nonprofit Boards 1993).

MARIE MALARO, A LEGAL PRIMER ON MANAGING MUSEUM COLLECTIONS (Smithsonian Institute 1998).

JUDITH GRUMMON NELSON, SIX TIPS TO RECRUITING, OPERATING AND INVOLVING NONPROFIT BOARD MEMBERS (National Center for Nonprofit Boards 1991).

Symposium, *Bishop Estate Matter*, 21 U. HAW. L. REV. (2001).

ALAN D. ULLBERG & PATRICIA ULLBERG, MUSEUM TRUSTEESHIP (American Association of Museums 1981).

Case Law

Lynch v. John M. Redfield Found., 88 Cal. Rptr. 86 (Cal. Ct. App. 1970).

Mile-O-Mo Fishing Club, Inc. v. Noble, 210 N.E.2d 12 (Ill. App. Ct. 1965).

George Pepperdine Found. v. Pepperdine, 271 P.2d 600 (Cal. Ct. App. 1954).

Scheuer Family Found., Inc. v. 61 Assocs., 582 N.Y.S.2d 662 (1992).

Statutory and Other Authority

REV. MODEL NONPROFIT CORP. ACT §§ 8.30, 8.33, 8.41–8.42 (1988).

CAL. CORP. CODE §§ 5230–5231 (West 1991).

N.Y. NOT-FOR-PROFIT CORP. LAW § 717.719 (McKinney 1997).

Directors' and Officers' Insurance

Bibliography

JOHN A. EDIE, DIRECTORS AND OFFICERS LIABILITY INSURANCE AND INDEMNIFICATION (Council on Foundations 1988).

DAVID M. GISHE & VICKI E. FISHMAN, DIRECTORS AND OFFICERS LIABILITY INSURANCE OVERVIEW (2000).

Discrimination

Case Law

McGlatten v. Connally, 338 F. Supp. 448 (D.C. Cir. 1972).

New York State Club Assoc. v. City of New York, 487 U.S. 1 (1988).

Internet Sites

U.S. Department of Labor, Office of Small Business Programs (contains information to assist small business companies in complying with rules, regulations, and laws enforced by the U.S. Department of Labor), <http://www.dol.gov/dol/osbp/public/sbrefa/>.

Duty of Obedience

Bibliography

Jaclyn A. Cherry, *Update, The Current State of Nonprofit Director Liability*, 37 DUQ. L. REV. 557, 562 (Summer 1999).

JAMES J. FISHMAN & STEPHEN SCHWARZ, NONPROFIT ORGANIZATIONS 230 (2d ed. 2000).

Jill S. Manny, *Governance Issues for Nonprofit Religious Organizations*, 40 CATH. LAW. 1 (Summer 2000).

Case Law

In the Matter of the Manhattan Eye, Ear and Throat Hosp. v. Spitzer, 715 N.Y.S.2d 575 (Sup. Ct. 1999).

Effective Boards

Bibliography

REPORT OF THE BLUE RIBBON COMMISSION ON BOARD EVALUATION: IMPROVING DIRECTOR EFFECTIVENESS (National Association of Corporate Directors 2001).

ALVIN FREDERICK ZANDLER, MAKING BOARDS EFFECTIVE: THE DYNAMICS OF NONPROFIT GOVERNING BOARDS (Jossey-Bass 1999).

Employment Practices

Bibliography

WILLIAM J. QUIRK, HIRING HANDBOOK (Panel Publishers 1994).

JEREMY RIFKIN & ROBERT HEILBRONER, THE END OF WORK: THE DECLINE OF THE GLOBAL LABOR FORCE AND THE DAWN OF THE POST-MARKET ERA (1995).

Ethics

Bibliography

ANTHONY ADAIR, CODE OF CONDUCT FOR NGOs—A NECESSARY REFORM (Institute of Economic Affairs 1999).

Nonprofit Organization Ethics, ASSOCIATION MANAGEMENT, April 1995.

Fiduciary Duties

Bibliography

DAVID W. BARRETT, A CALL FOR MORE LENIENT DIRECTOR LIABILITY STANDARDS FOR SMALL CHARITABLE NONPROFIT CORPORATIONS (Trustees of Indiana University 1996).

JAMES C. BAUGHMAN, TRUSTEES, TRUSTEESHIP AND THE PUBLIC GOOD (1987).

Harvey Goldschmid, *The Fiduciary Duties of Nonprofit Directors and Officers: Paradoxes, Problems and Proposed Reforms*, 23 IOWA J. CORP. L. 4, 631–653 (1998).

Financial

Bibliography

HERRINGTON J. BRYCE, FINANCIAL AND STRATEGIC MANAGEMENT FOR NONPROFIT ORGANIZATIONS (2d ed. 1992).

JOHN PAUL DALSIMER, UNDERSTANDING NONPROFIT FINANCIAL STATEMENTS: A PRIMER FOR BOARD MEMBERS (National Center for Nonprofit Boards 1996).

FINANCIAL MANAGEMENT FOR NONPROFIT ORGANIZATIONS (Tracy D. Connors and Christopher T. Callaghan, eds., 1982).

JO ANN HANKIN, ALAN G. SEIDNER & JOHN T. ZIETLOW, FINANCIAL MANAGEMENT FOR NONPROFIT ORGANIZATIONS (1998).

BEVIS LONGSTRETH, MODERN INVESTMENT MANAGEMENT AND THE PRUDENT MAN RULE (1986).

JEROME B. MCKINNEY, EFFECTIVE FINANCIAL MANAGEMENT IN PUBLIC AND NONPROFIT AGENCIES, 2ND EDITION (1995).

Form 990

Bibliography

Evelyn Brody, *A Taxing Time for the Bishop Estate: What Is the I.R.S. Role in Charity Governance?*, 21 HAWAII L. REV. 537 (1999).

ANDREW S. LANG & MICHAEL SORRELLS, THE IRS FORM 990: A WINDOW INTO NONPROFITS (National Center for Nonprofit Boards 2001).

Internet Sites

Guidestar®, The National Database of Nonprofit Organizations (posts copies of Form 990), <http://www.guidestar.org>.

Formation

Bibliography

JOHN A. EDIE, FIRST STEPS IN STARTING A FOUNDATION (4th ed., Council on Foundations 1987).

Harry G. Henn & Michael George Pfeifer, *Nonprofit Groups: Factors Influencing Choice of a Form*, 11 WAKE FOREST L. REV. 181 (June 1975).

BRUCE HOPKINS, STARTING AND MANAGING A NONPROFIT ORGANIZATION: A LEGAL GUIDE (3d ed. 2001).

PLANNING TAX-EXEMPT ORGANIZATIONS (Robert J. Desiderio & Scott A. Taylor, eds., Shephard's McGraw Hill Treatise, updated annually in loose-leaf form, 1984).

Case Law

Lynch v. Spilman, 431 P.2d 636 (Cal. 1987).

Queen of Angeles Hospital v. Younger, 136 Cal. Rptr. 36 (Cal. Ct. App. 1977).

Statutory and Other Authority

REVISED MODEL NONPROFIT CORP. ACT § 202 (1988).

CAL. CORP. CODE § 5130 (West 1991).

Foundations

Bibliography

FRANK EMERSON ANDREWS, PHILANTHROPIC GIVING (SAGE PUBLICATIONS 1950).

JOHN A. EDIE, FIRST STEPS IN STARTING A FOUNDATION (Foundation Center 1993).

FOUNDATION CENTER, THE FOUNDATION DIRECTORY, 2002 EDITION (23rd ed., 2002).

FOUNDATION CENTER, FOUNDATION GIVING 2002 (2002).

Peter Franklin, *Fidelity in Philanthropy: Two Challenges to Community Foundations*, NONPROFIT MANAGEMENT & LEADERSHIP, Fall 1997, at 65.

DAVID F. FREEMAN, THE HANDBOOK ON PRIVATE FOUNDATIONS (rev. ed., Council on Foundations 1991).

BRUCE R. HOPKINS & JUDY BLAZEK, PRIVATE FOUNDATIONS: TAX LAW AND COMPLIANCE (Wiley 2002).

WALDEMAR A. NIELSON, THE BIG FOUNDATIONS, Reprint Edition (Columbia University Press, 1972).U.S. Treasury Department, Internal Revenue Service. Tax Information for Private Foundations and Foundation Managers. Publication No. 578.

Fund Raising

Bibliography

DAVID G. BAUER, THE HOW TO GRANTS MANUAL: SUCCESSFUL GRANT-SEEKING TECHNIQUES FOR OBTAINING PUBLIC AND PRIVATE GRANTS (4th ed. 1999).

MICHAEL E. BURNS, PROPOSAL WRITER'S GUIDE (Development & Technical Assistance Center 1989).

MIM CARLSON, WINNING GRANTS STEP BY STEP: SUPPORT CENTERS OF AMERICA (1995).

SORAYA M. COLEY & CYNTHIA SCHEINBERG, PROPOSAL WRITING (Sage Publications 2000).

FOUNDATION CENTER, GUIDE TO PROPOSAL WRITING (rev. ed. 1997).

ELEANOR G. GILPATRICK, GRANTS FOR NONPROFIT ORGANIZATIONS: A GUIDE TO FUNDING AND GRANT WRITING (1989).

JUDITH MIRICK GOOCH, WRITING WINNING PROPOSALS (Council for Advancement and Support of Education 1987).

JAMES M. GREENFIELD, FUND RAISING FUNDAMENTALS: A GUIDE TO ANNUAL GIVING FOR PROFESSIONALS AND VOLUNTEERS (1994).

MARY S. HALL, GETTING FUNDED: A COMPLETE GUIDE TO PROPOSAL WRITING (3d ed., Continuing Education Publications 1988).

FISHER HOWE, WHAT EVERY BOARD MEMBER SHOULD KNOW ABOUT FUNDRAISING (Jossey-Bass 1995).

NORTON J. KIRITZ, PROGRAM PLANNING AND PROPOSAL WRITING (expanded version, The Grantsmanship Center 1988).

JAMES GREGORY LORD, THE RAISING OF MONEY: THIRTY-FIVE ESSENTIALS EVERY TRUSTEE SHOULD KNOW (Third Sector Press 1983).

JUDITH NICHOLS, PINPOINTING AFFLUENCE IN THE 21ST CENTURY: INCREASING YOUR SHARE OF MAJOR DONOR DOLLARS (Bonus Books 2001).

TERESA OHENDAHL, CHARITY BEGINS AT HOME: GENEROSITY AND SELF-INTEREST AMONG THE PHILANTHROPIC ELITE (1990).

JOHN SIMON, CHARLES POWERS & JON GUNNEMANN, THE ETHICAL INVESTORS: UNIVERSITIES AND CORPORATE RESPONSIBILITY (Yale University Press 1972).

Case Law

Riley v. National Federation of the Blind, 487 U.S. 781 (1988).

Young v. New York City Transit Auth., 903 F.2d 146 (2d Cir. 1990), *cert. denied*, 498 U.S. 984 (1990).

General

Bibliography

BETSY BUCHALTER ADLER, THE RULES OF THE ROAD, A GUIDE TO THE LAW OF CHARITIES IN THE UNITED STATES (Council on Foundations 1999).

Jennifer Alexander, *The Impact of Devolution on Nonprofits: A Multiphase Study of Social Services Organizations*, NONPROFIT MANAGEMENT AND LEADERSHIP, Fall 1999, at 57.

AMERICA'S WEALTHY AND THE FUTURE OF FOUNDATIONS (Teresa Odendahl, ed., 1987).

ROBERT C. ANADTINGA & TODD W. ENGSTROM, NONPROFIT BOARD ANSWER BOOK (National Center for Nonprofit Boards 2001).

JAMES T. BENNETT AND THOMAS J. DILORENZO, UNHEALTHY CHARITIES (Basic Books 1994).

VICTORIA B. BJORKLUND ET AL., NEW YORK NONPROFIT LAW AND PRACTICE WITH TAX ANALYSIS (1997).

R. BLANKEN & A. LIFF, FACING THE FUTURE: PREPARING YOUR ASSO-CIATION TO THRIVE (American Society of Association Executives Foundation 1999).

GEORGE G. BOGERT & GEORGE T. BOGERT, THE LAW OF TRUSTS AND TRUSTEES (2d rev. ed. 1991).

DANIEL J. BOORSTIN, FROM CHARITY TO PHILANTHROPY (Harper & Row 1987).

BOSTON COLLEGE SOCIAL WELFARE RESEARCH INSTITUTE, MILLIONAIRES AND THE MILLENNIUM: NEW ESTIMATES OF THE FORTHCOMING WEALTH TRANSFER AND THE PROSPECTS FOR A GOLDEN AGE OF PHILANTHROPY (1999), *available at* <http://www.bc.edu/swri>.

Robert O. Bothwell & Elizabeth Wiener, *Trends in Corporate Reporting on Philanthropic Efforts,* in THE FUTURE OF THE NONPROFIT SECTOR. (Virginia Hodgkinson, Richard Lyman & Associates, eds., Jossey-Bass 1989).

WILLIAM G. BOWEN, THOMAS I. NYGREN, SARAH E. TURNER & ELIZABETH A. DUFFY, THE CHARITABLE NONPROFITS: AN ANALYSIS OF INSTITUTIONAL DYNAMICS AND CHARACTERISTICS (Jossey-Bass 1990).

ROBERT HAMLETT BREMNER, AMERICAN PHILANTHROPY (University of Chicago 1990).

David A. Brennan, *The Power of the Treasury: Racial Discrimination, Public Policy and Charity in Contemporary Society,* 33 U.C. DAVIS L. REV. 389 (2000).

ELEANOR L. BRILLIANT, PRIVATE CHARITY AND PUBLIC INQUIRY: A HISTORY OF THE FILER AND PETERSON COMMISSIONS (Indiana University Press 2001).

Evelyn Brody, *Agents Without Principals: The Economic Convergence of the Nonprofit and For-Profit Organizational Forms,* 40 N.Y.L. SCH. L. REV. 457 (1996).

Louis J. Budd, *Altruism Arrives in America in* THE AMERICAN CULTURE (Hennig Cohen ed., 1968).

CAPACITY FOR CHANGE: THE NON-PROFIT WORLD IN THE AGE OF DEVOLUTION (Dwight F. Burlingame et. al., eds., Indiana University Center of Philanthropy 1996).

DAVID CANNADINE, DECLINE AND FALL OF BRITISH ARISTOCRACY ch. 5 (Vintage 1999).

GERALD CELENTE, TRENDS 2000: HOW TO PREPARE FOR CHANGES OF THE 21ST CENTURY (Warner Brothers 1997).

Charles T. Clotfelter, Symposium, What is Charity? Implications for Law and Policy, *Tax-Induced Distortions in the Voluntary Sector,* 39 CASE W. RES. L. REV. 663 (1988–89).

CHARLES T. CLOTFELTER, WHO BENEFITS FROM THE NONPROFIT SECTOR? (Univ. of Chicago Press 1992).

CHARLES T. CLOTFELTER & THOMAS EHRLICH, PHILANTHROPY AND THE NONPROFIT SECTOR IN A CHANGING AMERICA (Indiana University Press 1999).

LILLY COHEN AND DENNIS R. YOUNG, CAREERS FOR DREAMERS AND DOERS: A GUIDE TO MANAGEMENT CAREERS IN THE NONPROFIT SECTOR (The Foundation Center 1989).

CORPORATE PHILANTHROPY AT THE CROSSROADS (Dwight Burlingame & Dennis Young, eds. 1996).

Merle Curti, *American Philanthropy and the National Character*, 10 AMERICAN QUARTERLY 420, 420–37 (1958).

ALEXIS DE TOCQUEVILLE, DEMOCRACY IN AMERICA (P. Bradley Edition, Alfred A. Knopf 1966).

Peter F. Drucker, *The Age of Social Transformation*, Atlantic Monthly, November 1994, at 53.

PETER F. DRUCKER, MANAGING FOR THE FUTURE: THE 1990S AND BEYOND (Truman Talley Books/Dutton 1992).

PAUL B. FIRSTENBERG, MANAGING FOR PROFIT IN THE NONPROFIT WORLD (The Foundation Center 1986).

PAUL B. FIRSTENBERG, THE 21ST CENTURY NONPROFIT: REMAKING THE ORGANIZATION IN THE POST-GOVERNMENT ERA (The Foundation Center 1996).

James J. Fishman, *The Development of Nonprofit Corporation Law and an Agenda for Reform*, 34 EMORY L.J. 617 (Summer & Fall 1985).

JAMES J. FISHMAN & STEPHEN SCHWARZ, NONPROFIT ORGANIZATIONS: CASES AND MATERIALS (Foundation Press 2000).

MARION R. FREMONT-SMITH, PHILANTHROPY AND THE BUSINESS CORPORATION (Russell Sage Foundation 1972).

John W. Gardner, *Foreword* to BRIAN O'CONNOR, AMERICA'S VOLUNTARY SPIRIT (Foundation Center 1983).

GILBERT M. GAUL & NEIL A. BOROWSKI, FREE RIDE: THE TAX EXEMPT ECONOMY (Andrews and McMeel 1993).

Kara A. Gilmore, *House Bill No. 1095: The New Nonprofit Corporation Law for Missouri*, 63 U. MO. K.C. L. REV. 633 (1995).

SANDRA TRICE GRAY, EVALUATION WITH POWER: A NEW APPROACH TO ORGANIZATIONAL EFFECTIVENESS, EMPOWERMENT, AND EXCELLENCE (Independent Sector & Jossey-Bass 1997).

KEVIN M. GUTHRIE, THE NEW YORK HISTORICAL SOCIETY—LESSONS LEARNED FROM ONE NONPROFIT'S LONG-TERM STRUGGLE FOR SURVIVAL (Jossey-Bass 1996).

PETER DOBKIN HALL, INVENTING THE NONPROFIT SECTOR AND OTHER ESSAYS ON PHILANTHROPY, VOLUNTARISM, AND NONPROFIT ORGANIZATIONS (Johns Hopkins 1992).

Peter Dobkin Hall, Private Philanthropy and Public Policy: A Historical Appraisal (1992).

Henry B. Hansmann, *Reforming Nonprofit Corporation Law*, 129 U. Pa. L. Rev. 497 (1981).

Henry B. Hansmann, *The Role of Nonprofit Enterprise*, 89 Yale L.J. 835 (1980).

Henry B. Hansmann, Symposium, What Is Charity? Implications for Law and Policy, *The Evolving Law of Nonprofit Organizations: Do Current Trends Make Good Policy?*, 39 Case W. Res. L. Rev. 807 (1988–89).

James Edward Harris, The Nonprofit Corporation Act of 1993: Considering the Election to Apply the New Law to Old Corporations (Board of Trustees of the Univ. of Arkansas 1994).

Regina E. Herzlinger, *Can Public Trust in Nonprofits and Governments Be Restored?*, Harv. Bus. Rev., March-April 1996, at 98.

Alan G. Hevesy & Ira Millstein, Nonprofit Governance in New York City (2001).

Gertrude Himmelfarb, Poverty and Compassion: The Moral Imagination of the Late Victorians (Vintage 1991).

Virginia A. Hodgkinson and Richard W. Lyman, eds., The Future of the Nonprofit Sector (Jossey-Bass 1989).

Michael C. Hone, Symposium, What Is Charity? Implications for Law and Policy, *Aristotle and Lyndon Baines Johnson: Thirteen Ways of Looking at Blackbirds and Nonprofit Corporations—The American Bar Association's Revised Model Nonprofit Corporation Act* 39 Case W. Res. L. Rev. 751 (1888–89).

Bruce Hopkins, A Legal Guide to Starting and Managing a Nonprofit Organization (2d ed., John Wiley & Sons 1993).

Bruce R. Hopkins, The Law of Tax Exempt Organizations (7th ed., John Wiley & Sons 1998).

Jerald A. Jacobs, *Introduction* to American Bar Association Revised Model Nonprofit Corporation Act, (Prentice Hall Law & Business 1988).

Mary A. Jacobson, *Commentary* to *Recent Developments in Delaware Corporate Law: Nonprofit Corporations: Conversion to For-Profit Corporate Status & Nonprofit Corporation Members' Rights—Farahpour v. DCX, Inc., DE Law School of Widener Univ. Inc., 1995.

Leading for Innovation and Organizing for Results (Frances Hesselbein, Marshall Goldsmith, & Iain Somerville, eds., The Peter F. Drucker Foundation and Jossey-Bass 2001).

Kenneth D. Lewis, Jr., Casenote & Comment, *The Ramifications of Idaho's New Uniform Unincorporated Nonprofit Associations Act*, 31 IDAHO L. REV. 297 (1994).

RICHARD W. LYMAN, WHAT KIND OF SOCIETY SHOULD WE HAVE? (Acumen Fund 2001).

PAMELA A. MANN, CURRENT ISSUES IN ADVISING NONPROFIT ORGANIZATIONS (Practicing Law Institute 1998).

KATHLEEN D. MCCARTHY, NOBLESSE OBLIGE: CHARITY AND CULTURAL PHILANTHROPY IN CHICAGO 1848-1929 (University of Chicago 1982).

MAKING THE NONPROFIT SECTOR IN THE UNITED STATES: A READER (David Harmach, ed., Indiana University Press 1998).

THOMAS NAGEL, THE POSSIBILITY OF ALTRUISM (Oxford 1970).

WALDEMAR A. NIELSEN, THE THIRD SECTOR: KEYSTONE OF A CARING SOCIETY (Acumen Fund 2001).

THE NONPROFIT SECTOR: A RESEARCH HANDBOOK (Walter W. Powell, ed., Yale 1987).

BRIAN O'CONNELL, AMERICA'S VOLUNTARY SPIRIT: A BOOK OF READINGS (The Foundation Center 1983).

HOWARD L. OLECK, NONPROFIT CORPORATIONS, ORGANIZATIONS, AND ASSOCIATIONS (5th ed. 1988).

MICHAEL O'NEILL, THE THIRD AMERICA: THE EMERGENCE OF THE NONPROFIT SECTOR IN THE UNITED STATES (1989).

THE ORGANIZATION OF THE FUTURE (Frances Hesselbein, et al, eds., Jossey-Bass 1997).

FRANCIS OSTROWER, WHY THE WEALTHY GIVE: THE CULTURE OF ELITE PHILANTHROPY (1995).

ROBERT PAYTON ET AL., PHILANTHROPY: FOUR VIEWS (1988).

PHILANTHROPIC GIVING: STUDIES IN VARIETIES AND GOALS (Richard Magat, ed., Oxford University Press 1989).

ROBERT D. PUTNAM, BOWLING ALONE (Simon & Schuster 2000).

THE RESPONSIBILITIES OF WEALTH (Dwight Burlingame ed., Indiana University Press 1992).

WILLIAM P. RYAN, HIGH PERFORMANCE NONPROFIT ORGANIZATIONS: MANAGING UPSTREAM FOR GREATER PROFIT (John Wiley & Sons 1998).

Albert M. Sacks, *The Role of Philanthropy: An Institutional View*, 46 VA. L. REV. 516 (1960).

LESTER M. SALAMON, AMERICA'S NONPROFIT SECTOR (The Foundation Center 1999).

LESTER M. SALAMON, THE EMERGING NONPROFIT SECTOR: AN OVERVIEW (St. Martin's Press 1996).

LESTER M. SALAMON, PARTNERS IN PUBLIC SERVICE (Johns Hopkins University Press 1995).

Joseph A. Schumpeter, *Developments in the Law—Nonprofit Corporations*, 105 HARV. L. REV. 1579 (1992).

Austin W. Scott & William F. Fratcher, IV, Scott on Trusts (4th ed. 1989).

MICHAEL SELTZER, SECURING YOUR ORGANIZATION'S FUTURE: A COMPLETE GUIDE TO FUND RAISING STRATEGIES (rev. ed., The Foundation Center 2001).

Michael G. Sem, Note, *Szarzynski v. YMCA—Camp Minikani: Protecting Nonprofit Organizations from Liability under the Recreational Use Statute*, 184 WIS. L. REV. 1209 (1995).

NORMAN I. SILBER, A CORPORATE FORM OF FREEDOM—THE EMERGENCE OF THE NONPROFIT SECTOR (Westview 2000).

Hayden W. Smith, *Corporate Contributions to the Year 2000: Growth or Decline?, in* THE FUTURE OF THE NONPROFIT SECTOR: CHALLENGES, CHANGES, AND POLICY CONSIDERATIONS (Virginia A. Hodgkinson and Richard W. Lyman eds., 1989).

STEVEN SMITH AND MICHAEL LIPSKY, NONPROFITS FOR HIRE: THE WELFARE STATE IN THE AGE OF CONTRACTING (Harvard University Press 1995).

THE SYSTEMS AUDIT GROUP, INC., DISASTER RECOVERY YELLOW PAGES (Stephen Lewis ed. 1998).

RICHARD TITMUSS, THE GIFT RELATIONSHIP (1970).

GARY A. TOBIN, AMERICAN JEWISH PHILANTHROPY IN THE 1990S (Brandeis University Press 1995).

UNITED WAY OF PENNSYLVANIA, THE PENNSYLVANIA NON-PROFIT HANDBOOK (Non-Profit Advocacy Network 1992).

VISION AND VALUES: RETHINKING THE NONPROFIT SECTOR IN AMERICA (Deborah Gardner, ed., The Nathan Cummings Foundation 1998).

Warren Weaver, *Pre-Christian Philanthropy in* AMERICA'S VOLUNTARY SPIRIT at 5 (Brian O'Connell 1983).

BURTON WEISBROD, THE NONPROFIT ECONOMY (1988).

THOMAS WOLF, MANAGING A NONPROFIT ORGANIZATION (Prentice-Hall 1990).

DANIEL YERGIN & JOSEPH STANISLAW, THE COMMANDING HEIGHTS: THE BATTLE BETWEEN GOVERNMENT AND THE MARKETPLACE THAT IS REMAKING THE MODERN WORLD (Simon & Schuster Books 1998).

Case Law

Redlands Surgical Serv. v. Commissioner, 113 T.C. 3 (1999).

Statutory and Other Authority

U.S. CONST., amend. I, V, XIV.

S. 1622, 83d Cong., 2nd Session (1954).

CAL. CORP. CODE §§ 5142, 5230–5231, 5250, 6215–16, 6320–23, 6330–34, 6511, 6811–14, 9230 (West 1991).

Delaware Corp. Law § 102 (McKinney 2000).

N.Y. BUS. CORP. LAW § 402 (McKinney 1986).

N.Y. BUS. CORP. LAW § 707 (McKinney 1986).

N.Y. BUS. CORP. LAW § 708(d) (McKinney 1986).

N.Y. NOT-FOR-PROFIT CORP. LAW §§ 102, 201, 202, 205, 401-406, 519-522, 601, 621, 701-727 (McKinney 1997 Supp. 2001).

Internet Sites

BoardSource (formerly National Center for Nonprofit Boards, a resource for practical information, tools and best practices, training, and leadership development for board members of nonprofit organizations worldwide), <http://www.boardsource.org>.

The Business Roundtable (an association of CEOs committed to improving public policy), <http://www.brtable.org>.

The Chronicle of Higher Education (weekly news and job-information source for college and university faculty members, administrators, and staff), <http://www.chronicle.com>.

The Chronicle of Philanthropy (bi-weekly news source for charity leaders, fund raisers, and other people involved in the philanthropic enterprise), <http://www.philanthropy.com>.

Institute for Not-for-Profit Management, Columbia University Business School (offers graduate programs that help students develop effective management and leadership techniques for nonprofit organizations), <http://www.gsb.columbia.edu/exceed/INM/index.html>.

Internet Nonprofit Center (publishes the Nonprofit FAQ, a resource of information provided by partcipants in many online discussions about nonprofits and their work), <http://www.nonprofits.org>.

Mandel Center for Nonprofit Organizations, Case Western Reserve University (a multidisciplinary center for education, research, and community service, also offers graduate programs for nonprofit leaders and managers), <http://www.cwru.edu/mandelcenter>.

National Associations of Corporate Secretaries (includes efficient access to helpful information regarding its publications and seminars), <http://www.nacsonline.org>.

NATIONAL COMMISSION ON PHILANTHROPY AND CIVIC RENEWAL, GIVING BETTER, GIVING SMARTER: RENEWING PHILANTHROPY IN AMERICA (1997), *available at* <http://www.hudson.org/ncpcr/report/report.html>.

Program on Non-Profit Organizations, The Yale Divinity School (an international center for multidisciplinary studies of philanthropy, voluntarism, and nonprofit organizations), <http://www.yale.edu/divinity/ponpo>.

Spencer Stuart (provides executive search and other human resources consulting services), <http://www.spencerstuart.com>.

Governance

Bibliography

LESLIE A. ABBEY, CORPORATE GOVERNANCE: A GUIDE FOR NOT-FOR-PROFIT DIRECTORS (1996).

A.C.G., *The Fiduciary Duties of Loyalty and Care Associated with the Directors and Trustees of Charitable Organizations*, 64 VA. L. REV. 449 (April 1978).

AMERICAN SOCIETY OF CORPORATE SECRETARIES, CORPORATE GOVERNANCE PRINCIPLES: A REPRESENTATIVE SAMPLING (1998).

AMERICAN SOCIETY OF CORPORATE SECRETARIES, THE CORPORATE SECRETARY AND THE BOARD OF DIRECTORS: A COMPREHENSIVE GUIDEBOOK (1987).

AMERICAN SOCIETY OF CORPORATE SECRETARIES, CURRENT BOARD PRACTICES, 4TH STUDY (2002).

AMERICAN SOCIETY OF CORPORATE SECRETARIES & NATIONAL CENTER FOR NONPROFIT BOARDS, GOVERNANCE FOR NONPROFITS: FROM LITTLE LEAGUE TO UNIVERSITIES (1998).

WILLIAM G. BOWEN, INSIDE THE BOARDROOM: GOVERNANCE BY DIRECTORS AND TRUSTEES (John Wiley & Sons 1994).

Herrington J. Bryce, *The Fundamental Pillars of Nonprofit Governance*, DIRECTOR'S MONTHLY, Dec. 1999, at 12.

HERRINGTON J. BRYCE, THE NONPROFIT BOARD'S ROLE IN ESTABLISHING FINANCIAL POLICIES (National Center for Nonprofit Boards 1996).

JOHN CARVER, BOARDS THAT MAKE A DIFFERENCE: A NEW DESIGN FOR LEADERSHIP IN NONPROFIT AND PUBLIC ORGANIZATIONS (Jossey-Bass 1997).

Zechariah Chafee, *The Internal Affairs of Associations Not for Profit*, 43 HARV. L. REV. 993 (1930).

COMMISSION ON PRIVATE PHILANTHROPY AND PUBLIC NEEDS, GIVING IN AMERICA: TOWARD A STRONGER VOLUNTARY SECTOR (1975).

COMMITTEE ON CORPORATE LAWS, CORPORATE DIRECTOR'S GUIDEBOOK (American Bar Association 1994).

Peter F. Drucker, *Lessons for Successful Nonprofit Governance*, NONPROFIT MANAGEMENT & LEADERSHIP, Fall 1990, at 7.

PETER F. DRUCKER, MANAGEMENT: TASKS, RESPONSIBILITIES, PRACTICES (Harper & Row 1974).

PETER F. DRUCKER, MANAGING THE NONPROFIT ORGANIZATIONS (Harper Collins 1992).

FILER COMMISSION, U.S. DEPARTMENT OF THE TREASURY, COMMISSION ON PRIVATE PHILANTHROPY AND PUBLIC NEEDS: RESEARCH PAPERS, VOLUMES I-V (1977).

CYRIL O. HOULE, GOVERNING BOARDS: THEIR NATURE AND NURTURE (Jossey-Bass 1989).

DANIEL L. KURTZ, BOARD LIABILITY (Moyer Bell Limited 1988).

BERIT M. LAKEY, NONPROFIT GOVERNANCE: STEERING YOUR ORGANIZATION WITH AUTHORITY AND ACCOUNTABILITY (National Center for Nonprofit Boards 2000).

GUIDEBOOK FOR DIRECTORS OF NONPROFIT CORPORATIONS 2nd ed. (George W. Overton and Jeannie Carmedelle Frey eds., American Bar Association 2002).

Lisa A. Runquist, *A Job Description for Directors*, BUS. LAW TODAY, Nov.-Dec. 1994, at 10.

LISA A. RUNQUIST, RESPONSIBILITIES AND DUTIES OF A DIRECTOR OF A NONPROFIT ORGANIZATION (Maxwell-MacMillan Charitable Giving and Solicitations Service 1995).

GREGORY V. VARALLO & DANIEL A. DREISBACH, FUNDAMENTALS OF CORPORATE GOVERNANCE (American Bar Association 1996).

THOMAS WOLF, MANAGING A NONPROFIT ORGANIZATION (Prentice-Hall 1990).

Case Law

Aramony v. United Way of America, 28 F. Supp. 2d 147 (S.D.N.Y. 1993).

Branude v. Havenner, 113 Cal. Rptr. 386 (Cal. Ct. App. 1971).

Holt v. College of Osteopathic Physicians and Surgeons, 394 P.2d 932 (Cal. 1964).

Nixon v. Lichtenstein, 959 S.W.2d 854 (Mo. Ct. App. 1997).

Stern v. Lucy Webb Hayes Nat'l Training School for Deaconesses, 381 F. Supp. 1003 (D.C. 1974). (Sibley Hospital Case).

Statutory and Other Authority

Rev. Model Nonprofit Corp. Act § 10.31 (1988).

Internet Sites

Alliance for Nonprofit Management (devoted to improving the management and governance capacity of nonprofits), <http://www.allianceonline.org>.

Corporate Governance (focuses on nonprofit corporate governance topics for stakeholders), <http://www.corpgov.net>.

Leader to Leader (the Drucker Foundation's quarterly journal offering articles on leadership, management, and strategy), <http://drucker.org/leaderbooks/index.html>.

Health Care, Hospitals

Bibliography

Phillip P. Biesi, Comment, *Conversion of Nonprofit Health Care Entities to For-Profit Status,* 26 Cap. U. L. Rev. 805 (1997).

Andréa I. Castro, Comment, *Overview of the Tax Treatment of Nonprofit Hospitals and Their For-Profit Subsidiaries: A Short-Sighted View Could be Very Bad Medicine,* 15 Pace L. Rev. 501 (Winter 1995).

Robert Charles Clark, *Does the Nonprofit Form Fit the Hospital Industry?,* 93 Harv. L. Rev. 1416 (1980).

Kevin F. Donohue, *Crossroads in Hospital Conversions—A Survey of Nonprofit Hospital Conversion Legislation,* 8 Ann. Health L. 39 (1999).

N. Keith Emge, Jr., Note, *Nonprofit Hospitals and the State Tax Exemption: An Analysis of the Issues Since* Utah County v. Intermountain Health Care, Inc. 9 VA. TAX REV. 599, 599 (1990).

James J. Fishman, *Checkpoints on the Conversion Highway: Some Trouble Spots in the Conversion of Nonprofit Health Care Organizations to For-Profit Status*, 23 IOWA J. CORP. L. 701 (1998).

BARRY R. FURROW, SONDRA H. JOHNSON, TIMOTHY S. JOST & ROBERT L. SCHWARTZ, THE LAW OF HEALTH CARE ORGANIZATIONS AND FINANCE (1991).

David L. Glazer, Comment, *Clayton Act Scrutiny of Nonprofit Hospital Mergers: The Wrong Picture for Ailing Institutions*, 66 WASH. L. REV. 1041 (1991).

Shannon McGhee Hernandez, *Conversion of Nonprofit Hospitals to For-Profit Status: The Tennessee Experience*, 28 U. MEM. L. REV. 1077 (1998).

Melvin Horowitz, *Corporate Reorganization: The Last Gasp or the Last Clear Chance for the Tax-Exempt, Nonprofit Hospital?*, 13 AM J. L. & MED. 527 (1988).

Fust Krause, *Do No Harm: An Analysis of the Nonprofit Hospital Sale Act*, 45 UCLA L. REV. 503 (1997).

Theodore Marmor, Mark Schlesinger & Richard Smithley, *Nonprofit Organizations and Health Care in* THE NONPROFIT SECTOR: A RESEARCH HANDBOOK (W. Powell ed., 1987).

JULIO MATEO, JR. & JAIME ROSSI, WHITE KNIGHTS OR TROJAN HORSES— A POLICY FOR EVALUATING CONSOLIDATIONS IN CALIFORNIA, (Consumers Union West Coast Regional Office, 1999).

Vicenzo Stampone, Note, *Turning Patients into Profits: Nonprofit Hospital Conversions Spur Legislation*, 22 SETON HALL LEGIS J. 627 (1998).

Information Flow

Bibliography

Richard S. Maurer, *Director Information Systems: The Advance Information Package, Minutes and Corporate Reports, in* HAND-BOOK FOR CORPORATE DIRECTORS (R.R. Donnelley & Sons 1985).

John Mountjoy, *Information Flow to Directors, in* THE CORPORATE SECRETARY AND THE BOARD OF DIRECTORS: A COMPREHENSIVE GUIDEBOOK (American Society of Corporate Secretaries 1987).

Intermediate Sanctions

Bibliography

T. J. Sullivan, Kathleen Nilles, Ralph De Jong, Bernadette Broccolo & Michael Peregrine, *Temporary Intermediate Sanctions Regulations*, 31 EXEMPT ORG. TAX REV. 177 (Feb. 2001).

Case Law

Abraham Lincoln Opportunity Found. v. Commissioner, 2000 T.C.M. (RIA) § 2000-261 (2000).

International

Bibliography

ANTHONY ADAIR, A CODE OF CONDUCT FOR NGOS—A NECESSARY REFORM (The Institute of Economic Affairs 1999).

JOHN A. EDIE, BEYOND OUR BORDERS: A GUIDE TO MAKING GRANTS OUTSIDE THE U.S. COUNCIL ON FOUNDATIONS (2d ed. 1999).

JOHN A. EDIE & JANE C. NOBER, INTERNATIONAL GRANTMAKING: A REPORT ON U.S. FOUNDATION TRENDS (Foundations Center 1997).

Judith Miller, *Some Charities Suspected of Terrorist Role*, N.Y. TIMES, Feb. 19, 2000, at A5.

Statutory and Other Authority

I.R.B. 34 (1992).
I.R.C. §§ 509, 4945(h).
Rev. Proc. 92-94, 1992-46.

Internet Sites

Australian Agency for International Development (AusAID) (a Federal Government funded program working with other governments, Australian companies, non-government organizations, and individual experts to design and set up projects which tackle the causes and consequences of poverty in developing countries), <http://www.ausaid.gov.au>.

Charity Commission for England and Wales, (a statutory organization that regulates charities), <http://www.charity-commission. gov.uk/>.

Nonprofit Transformation Minnesota Council of Nonprofit Principles and Practices for Nonprofit Excellence (1998) (provides a survey of standards for charitable accountability), <http://www.avagara.com/ nonprof/accountability>.

U.S. International Grantmakers (provides access to recommended forms, country reports and laws, and other informational materials and resources), <http://www.usig.org>.

Internet

Bibliography

Reed Abelson, *ASE—Giving Sites Spring Up, Some Say It's Donors Beware*, N.Y. TIMES, Nov. 7, 1999, at C11.

FUND RAISING ON THE INTERNET, 2ND EDITION (Nick Allen, Ted Hart & Mal Warwick, eds., Jossey-Bass 2001).

Cheryl Chasin, Susan Ruth, & Robert Harper, *Tax Exempt Organizations and World Wide Web Fundraising and Advertising on the Internet*, EOCPE (for FY 2000) 119, available at <http://www.IRS.gov/bus_ info/eo/cpe.html>.

Ruth Chosin & Robert Harper, *Tax Exempt Organizations and World Wide Web Fundraising and Advertising on the Internet.* 9RS CPE MANUAL (1999).

Paul Demko, *On Line Solicitors: Tangled Web*, CHRONICLE OF PHILAN-THROPY, Jan. 29, 1998, at 23–24.

Holly Hall, *Tips on Deciding Whether Your Charity Should Be Listed on Giving Web Sites*, CHRON. OF PHILANTHROPY, June 15, 2000, at 39.

Pamela O'Kane Foster, *Lobbying on the Internet and the Internal Revenue Code's Regulation of Charitable Organizations*, 43 N.Y.L. SCH. L. REV. 567 (1999).

Christina L. Nooney, *Tax Exempt Organizations and the Internet*, 27 EXEMPT ORG. TAX REV. 33 (2000).

Statutory and Other Authority

I.R.C. § 6104(d)–(e) (2002); 26 C.F.R. § 301.6104(d)-2 (2002).
Ark. Code Ann. § 4-28-412 (Michie 1999).
Conn. Gen. Stat. § 21a-1-190h (1999).
Haw. Rev. Stat. § 467B-9 (1999).
Miss. Code Ann. § 79-11-519 (2000).
Or. Rev. Stat. § 128.856 (1999).
R.I. Gen. Laws § 5-53.1-7 (2000).

Internet Sites

National Association of State Charity Officials (NASCO) (allows regulators and enforcers of state charity laws to engage in ongoing dialogue with nonprofit leaders in the U.S. and around the world), <http://www.nasconet.org>.

Lobbying

Bibliography

Gregory L. Colvin & Lowell Finley, The Rules of the Game: An Election Year Legal Guide for Nonprofit Organizations (Alliance for Justice 1996).

Gail M. Harmon, Jessica A. Ladel & Eleanor A. Evans, Being a Player—A Guide to the IRS Lobbying Regulations for Advocacy Charities (The Advocacy Forum).

Independent Sector Playing by the Rules: Handbook on Voter Participation and Education Work for 501 (c)(3) Organizations, (1998).

League of Women Voters, Face to Face: A Guide to Candidate Debates (1996).

Bob Smucker, The Nonprofit Lobbying Guide, Second Edition (Independent Sector 1999).

John D. Sparks, Lobbying, Advocacy and Nonprofit Boards (National Center for Nonprofit Boards 1997).

Worry-Free Lobbying for Nonprofits: How to Use the 501(h) Election to Maximize Effectiveness (Alliance for Justice 2000).

Case Law

Christian Echoes Nat'l Ministry, Inc. v. United States, 470 F.2d 849
    (10th Cir. 1972).
Regan v. Taxation Without Representation of Washington, 461 U.S. 540
    (1983).

Statutory and Other Authority

I.R.C. § 527 (2002).

Internet Sites

Charity Lobbying in the Public Interest (a project of Independent
    Sector whose principal purpose is to educate charities about the
    important and appropriate role lobbying can play in achieving
    their missions), <http://www.clpi.org>.
Independent Sector (a national leadership forum fostering private ini-
    tiative for the public good), <http://www.independentsector.org>.
IRS, homepage for Internal Revenue Service, offers access to forms
    and publications as well as articles on tax-exempt organizations,
    <http://www.irs.gov>.
OMB Watch (monitors activities of the White House Office of Man-
    agement and Business, budget and governance performance
    issues, nonprofit advocacy and nonprofit policy and technology),
    <http://www.ombwatch.org>.

Marketing

Bibliography

Jerr Boschee, *Social Entrepreneurship: Transformation of Nonprofit
    Organizations into Social-Purpose Business Ventures,* ACROSS THE
    BOARD, March 1995 at 20.
J. Gregory Dees, *Enterprising Nonprofits,* HARVARD BUSINESS REVIEW,
    Jan.-Feb. 1998, at 55.
NEIL KOTLER & PHILIP KOTLER, MUSEUM STRATEGY AND MARKETING
    (Jossey-Bass 1998).

Philip Kotler & Harold T. Martin, *A Generic Concept of Marketing*, in INSIGHTS FOR MARKETING MANAGEMENT (Gabriel M. and Betsy D. Gelb, eds., Goodyear 1974).

Philip Kotler & Gerald Zaltman, *Social Marketing: An Approach to Planned Social Change*, J. OF MARKETING, Jan. 1969, at 33.

REBECCA K. LECT, MARKETING FOR MISSION (National Center for Nonprofit Boards 2001).

Membership Associations

Case Law

Bernstein v. Alameda-Contra Costa Med. Assoc., 293 P.2d 862 (Cal. Ct. App. 1956).

Dawkins v. Antrobus, 17 Ch. D. 615 (Ct. of App. 1881).

Falcone v. Middlesex County Med. Soc'y, 162 A.2d 324, *aff'd*, 170 A.2d 791 (N.J. 1961).

Lambert v. Fishermen's Dock Coop., Inc., 297 A.2d 566 (N.J. 1972).

Owen v. Rosicrucian Fellowship, 342 P.2d 424 (Cal. Ct. App. 1959).

Mergers and Consolidations

Bibliography

ANATOMY OF A MERGER: BJC HEALTH SYSTEM (Wayne M. Lerner ed., Health Administration Press 1997).

Statutory and Other Authority

GA. CODE ANN. § 14-3-1403 (2001).

MONT. CODE ANN. § 35-2-722 (2001).

N.Y. NOT-FOR-PROFIT CORP. LAW §§ 107, 1102(c), 12.02(g), 1403 (McKinney 1997).

TENN. CODE ANN. § 48-64-103 (1956).

Minutes

Bibliography

AMERICAN SOCIETY OF CORPORATE SECRETARIES, CORPORATE MINUTES: A MONOGRAPH FOR THE CORPORATE SECRETARY (1996).

Case Law

U.S. v. Rockford Mem'l Corp., 898 F.2d 1278 (7th Cir. 1990), *cert. denied*, 498 U.S. 920 (2002).

Mission Statements

Bibliography

JERR BOSCHEE, MERGING MISSION AND MONEY (National Center for Nonprofit Boards 1998).
PETER C. BRINKERHOFF, MISSION-BASED MANAGEMENT: LEADING YOUR NOT-FOR-PROFIT INTO THE 21ST CENTURY (Alpine Guild 1994).

Nominating Committee

Bibliography

AMERICAN SOCIETY OF CORPORATE SECRETARIES, NOMINATING COMMITTEE PRACTICES AND PROCEDURES (1981).

Case Law

Fitzgerald v. National Rifle Assoc., 383 F. Supp. 162 (D.N.J. 1974).

Orientation

Bibliography

Cyrus F. Freidheim, Preparing Your New Directors (Directors and Boards, Winter 1995).

Health Research and Education Trust, Welcome to the Board! An Orientation for the New Health Care Trustee (American Hospital Publishing 1999).

Stephanie R. Jovener, *The Value of Board Training,* in Corporate Law and Practice Course Handbook (Practicing Law Institute, Sept./Oct. 1999).

Private Foundations

Bibliography

Lauren Watson Cesare, Private Foundations and Public Charities—Definitions and Clarification (Tax Management 2000).

Records Retention

Bibliography

American Society of Corporate Secretaries, Records Retention (1985).

Internet Sites

Designing an Effective Records Retention Compliance Program (J. Edwin Dietel, J.D., ed., West Group-Clark Boardman Callaghan, Corporate Compliance Series, Volume 3), *available at* <http://www.westgroup.com>.

Disaster Recovery Yellow Pages (Steven Lewis, Ph.D., C.I.S.A., ed., The Systems Audit Group, Inc. 2002), *available at* <http://www.disaster-help.com>.

GUIDE TO RECORDS RETENTION (Business Laws, Inc. 2001), *available at* <http://www.businesslaws.com>.

RECORDS AND INFORMATION MANAGEMENT REPORT (Greenwood Publishing Group, Inc.) (explores solutions to information storage and retrieval problems while keeping records and documents managers current with new practices and technology) *available at* <http://www.greenwood.com/subscriber/rimr.htm>.

RECORDS RETENTION REPORT (Business Laws, Inc. (monthly report with suggestions on improving records retention)), *available at* <http://www.businesslaws.com>.

Registration

Bibliography

1 EXEMPT ORG. REP. (CCH) (full text of all state nonprofit corporation laws and laws governing charitable solicitations).

Case Law

Bensusan Restaurant Corp. v. Richard B. King, 126 F.3d 25 (2d Cir. 1997).

Cybersell, Inc. v. Cybersell, Inc., 130 F.3d 414 (9th Cir. 1997).

GTE New Media Serv. v. Bellsouth Corp., 199 F.3d 1343 (D.C. Cir. 2000).

Inset Sys. Inc. v. Instruction Set Inc., 937 F. Supp. 161 (D. Conn. 1996).

Maritz Inc. v. CyberGold, 947 F. Supp. 1338 (E.D. Mo. 1996).

Mink v. AAAA Development, LLC, 190 F.3d 333 (5th Cir. 1999).

Northern Lights Tech., Inc. v. Northern Lights Club, 97 F. Supp. 2d 96 (D. Ma. 2000).

Panavision International, L.P. v. Toeppen, 141 F.3d 1316, 1321 (9th Cir. 1998).

Quill Corp. v. North Dakota, 504 U.S. 298 (1992).

Zippo Mfg. Co. v. Zippo Dot Com, Inc., 952 F. Supp. 1119 (W.D. Pa. 1997).

Statutory and Other Authority

Rev. Model Nonprofit Corp. Act §§ 1.70, 16.22 (1988).

Fla. Stat. Ann. § 496.411 (West 2001).

Illinois Charitable Trust Act, 760 Ill. Comp. Stat. § 55/1–19 (2001).

Kan. Stat. Ann. § 17-1769 (2001).

Mich. Stat. Ann. § 450.2821 (Michie 2002).

Minn. Stat. § 501B.36 (1999).

Charitable Registration and Investigation Act, N.J. Stat. Ann. § 45:17A-24 (West 2001).

N.Y. Est. Powers & Trusts Law § 8-14 (McKinney 2001).

N.Y. Exec. Law § 172-d (McKinney 2001).

Internet Sites

Internet Nonprofit Center (contains telephone numbers, web sites and addresses of charities regulators in all states), <http://www.nonprofits.org/library/gov/urs>.

Religious Organizations

Bibliography

Trevor A. Brown, *Note Religious Nonprofits and the Commercial Manner Test* 99 Yale L. J. 1631 (1990).

Charles William Eliot, Views Respecting Present Exemption From Taxation of Property Used for Religious, Educational and Charitable Purposes (1974).

Independent Sector, From Belief to Commitment: The Community Service Activities and Resources of Religious Congregations in the United States (1993).

Fred Stokeld, *Church-State Watchdog Group Again on the Trail of Christian Coalition*, 26 Exempt Org. Tax Rev. 195 (Nov. 1999).

Fred Stokeld, *Virginia High Court to Hear University's Appeal on Exempt Bonds*, 28 Exempt Org. Tax Rev. 200 (May 2000).

Robert Wuthnow, Virginia Hodgkinson, et al., Faith and Philanthropy in America (Jossey-Bass 1990).

Case Law

Aguilar v. Felton, 473 U.S. 402 (1985).

American Guidance Found., Inc. v. United States, 490 F. Supp. 304 (1980).

Markus Q. Bishop, et ux. v. United States, 83 AFTR 2d Par. 99-815 (Mar. 18, 1999).

Branch Ministries Inc., et. al. v. Charles O. Rossotti, 40 F. Supp. 2d 15 (1999), *aff'd,* 211 F.3d 137 (2000).

Bubbling Wells Church of Universal Love, Inc. v. Commissioner, 74 T.C. 531 (1980), *aff'd,* 670 F.2d 104 (9th Cir. 1981).

Cantwell v. Connecticut, 310 U.S. 296 (1940).

Church by Mail, Inc. v. Commissioner, 765 F.2d 1387 (1985).

Church of Scientology of Cal. v. Commissioner, 823 F.2d 1310 (9th Cir. 1987).

City of Boerne v. Flores, 521 U.S. 507 (1997).

Eden v. Commissioner, 41 T.C. 605 (1964).

Eighth St. Baptist Church, Inc. v. United States, 291 F. Supp. 603 (1968), *aff'd,* 431 F.2d 1193 (1970).

Everson v. Board of Education, 330 U.S. 1 (1947).

Flowers v. United States, D.C., 82-1 USTC 9114 (1991).

Founding Church of Scientology v. United States, 412 F.2d 1197 (1969).

Hernandez v. Commissioner, 498 U.S. 680 (1989).

Holy Spirit Assoc. v. Tax Commission 55 N.Y. 2d 512 (1982).

Lemon v. Kurtzman, 403 U.S. 602 (1971).

Ling v. United States, 200 F. Supp. 282 (D.C. Minn. 1961).

Lutheran Social Serv. of Minnesota v. United States, 758 F.2d 1283 (8th Cir. 1985).

Meek v. Pittinger, 421 U.S. 349 (1975).

Henry W. Radde, et us. v. Commissioner, T.C. Memo 1997-490 (1997).

Serbian Eastern Orthodox Diocese v. Milivojevich 426 U.S. 696 (1976).

School District of the City of Grand Rapids v. Ball, 473 U.S. 373, 105 S. Ct. 3126 (1985).

Sherbert v. Verner, 374 U.S. 398 (1963).

Steele et al. v. Industrial Development Board of the Metropolitan Government of Nashville, et al., No. 3: 91-042 (M.D. Tenn., Oct. 24, 2000).

St. Martin Evangelical Lutheran Church v. U. South Dakota 451 U.S. 772 (1981).

Swaggart v. Calif. Equalization Bd., 493 U.S. 378 (1990).

Texas Monthly, Inc. v. Bob Bullock, Comptroller of Public Accounts of the State of Texas et. al., 488 U.S. 361, 109 S. Ct. 647 (1989).

United States v. Indianapolis Baptist Temple, et al., 86 AFTR 2d Par. 2000-5149 (7th Cir. Aug. 14, 2000).

Waltz v. Tax Commission, 397 U.S. 664, 669 (1970).

Warnke v. United States, 641 F. Supp. 1091 (1986).

Larry Whittington, et al. v. I.R.C., T.C. Memo 2000-96 (Sept. 21, 2000).

Statutory and Other Authority

I.R.C. §§ 115(a), 170(f), 401–403, 410(d), 414(e)(5), 501, 507, 508, 509, 1402, 3102, 3121, 3309, 3401, 3402, 4947(a)(1), 4947(a)(1), 4958, 6033, 6315, 7611 (1986).

I.R.S. Form 990-EZ, 990-PF, 1023, 1040, 8123, 8274.

I.R.S. Publication 517 (Social Security for Members of the Clergy and Religious Workers).

Priv. Ltr. Rul. 8519004 (Jan. 28, 1985).

Rev. Proc. 91-20, 1991-10 I.R.B. 26 (1991).

Rev. Rul. 70-549, 1970-2 C.B. 16 (1970).

Rev. Rul. 72-606, 1972-2 C.B. 78 (1972).

Rev. Rul. 79-78, 1971-1 C.B. 9 (1979).

Rev. Rul. 80-110, 1980-1 C.B. 190 (1980).

Treas. Reg. §§ 1.1402, 31.340.

Treas. Reg. §§ 1.501(3), 1.508-1(a)(3), 1.6033, 301-7611-1.

S. 1622, 83d Cong., 2nd Session (1954).

Employee Retirement Income Security Act, 29 U.S.C. §§ 33, 1002, 1003(b)(2), 1321(b)(3) (2002).

Religious Freedom Restoration Act, 42 U.S.C. §§ 2000bb et seq. (2002).

Religious Land Use and Institutionalized Persons Act of 2000, 42 U.S.C. §§ 2000cc et seq. (2002).

CAL. CORP. CODE § 9240(c) (West 1991).

Retreats

Bibliography

BARRY S. BADER, PLANNING SUCCESSFUL BOARD RETREATS: A GUIDE FOR BOARD MEMBERS AND CHIEF EXECUTIVES (National Center for Nonprofit Boards 1991).

Risk Management

Bibliography

JERALD JACOBS & DANIEL OGDEN, LEGAL RISK MANAGEMENT FOR ASSO-
CIATIONS (American Psychological Association 1995).

MARY LAI, ET AL., AM I COVERED FOR? (2d ed., Consortium for Human
Services, Inc. 1992).

RISK MANAGEMENT FOR NONPROFITS (2d ed., National Center for
Community Risk & Management Insurance 1992).

BYRON STONE & CAROL NORTH, RISK MANAGEMENT AND INSURANCE
FOR NONPROFIT MANAGER (First Non Profit Risk Pooling Trial,
Chicago, IL., 1988).

CHARLES TREMPER & GEORGE BABCOCK, THE NONPROFIT BOARD'S ROLE
IN RISK MANAGEMENT: MORE THAN BUYING INSURANCE (National
Center for Nonprofit Boards 1990).

Internet Sites

Nonprofit Risk Management Center (publications), <http://www.
nonprofitrisk.org>.

Search Firms

Bibliography

Elizabeth M. Fowler, *Recruiting for Nonprofit Boards*, N.Y. TIMES, Sept. 5,
1989, at D8.

Welton Jones, *Art Museum Trustees, Headhunters Labor over Criteria
for New Director*, SAN DIEGO TRIBUNE, Nov. 8, 1998, at E1.

Debra Nussbaum, *Earning It: Volunteer Reserves Get Harder To Sell*,
N.Y. TIMES, Jan. 14, 1996, at 3:10.

Jeanne B. Pinder, Big Business: Helping the Helpers, N.Y. TIMES, Nov.
18, 1998, at G8.

Nancy Polk, *Headhunters Try to Find a Heartbeat in Job Market*, N.Y.
TIMES, Dec. 6, 1992, at 13.

Lornet Turnbull, Search Firm Finds Booming Business Among City
Clients, COLUMBUS DISPATCH, Oct. 20, 1997, at 1D.

Internet Sites

Educational Management Network, Candidate Preview (executive
search firm serving education and nonprofit organizations),
<http://www.emnemn.com>.

Korn/Ferry International (provides recruitment solutions and management assessments), <http://www.kornferry.com>.

Spencer Stuart (a management consulting firm specializing in senior-level executive search and board director appointments), <http://www.spencerstuart.com>.

Standing

Case Law

In re Garrison, 137 A.2d 321 (Pa. 1958).

In re Lown, 59 Misc. 2d 987, 301 N.Y. S. 2d 746 (N.Y. Sur. 1969).

In re United States Catholic Conference, 885 F. 2d 1020 (2d Cir. 1989), *cert. denied*, 4954 U.S. 918 (1946). (Abortion Rights Mobilization Case)

Jones v. Grant, 344 So. 2d 1210 (Ala. 1977).

Matter of Rothko's Estate, 371 N.E. 2d 291 (N.Y. 1977).

McInnes v. Goldthwaite, 52 A.2d 795 (N.H. 1947).

Smithers v. St. Luke's Roosevelt Hosp. Ctr., 723 N.Y.S. 2d 426 (N.Y. App. Div. 2001).

Strategic Alliances

Bibliography

JAMES E. AUSTIN, THE COLLABORATION CHALLENGE: HOW NONPROFITS AND BUSINESSES SUCCEED THROUGH STRATEGIC ALLIANCES (Jossey-Bass 2000).

James E. Austin, *Principles for Partnership*, LEADER TO LEADER, Fall 2000, at 54.

ENTERPRISING NONPROFITS: A TOOLKIT FOR SOCIAL ENTREPRENEURS (J. Gregory Dees et al., eds. 2001).

LEADING BEYOND THE WALLS (Frances Hesselbein, Marshall Goldsmith & Vain Somerville, eds., Jossey-Bass 1999).

Christine W. Letts, William Ryan & Allen Grossman, *Virtuous Capital: What Foundations Can Learn from Venture Capitalists*, HARVARD BUSINESS REVIEW, Mar.-April 1997, at 36.

Strategic Planning

Bibliography

PETER C. BRINCHERHOFF, MISSION-BASED MANAGEMENT: LEADING YOUR NOT-FOR-PROFIT INTO THE 21ST CENTURY (Alpine Guild 1994).

BARRY W. BRYAN, STRATEGIC PLANNING WORKBOOK FOR NONPROFIT ORGANIZATIONS (Amherst H. Wilder Foundation 1986). PETER F. DRUCKER, HOW TO ASSESS YOUR NONPROFIT ORGANIZATION (1993).

Douglas C. Eadie, *Putting Vision to Powerful Use in Your Organization*, NONPROFIT WORLD, July-August 1995, at 40.

FISHER HOWE, A BOARD MEMBER'S GUIDE TO STRATEGIC PLANNING (Jossey-Bass 1997).

NEIL KOTLER & PHILIP KOTLER, MUSEUM STRATEGY AND MARKETING (Jossey-Bass 1998).

PHILIP KOTLER & A.R. ANDREASEN, STRATEGIC MARKETING FOR NONPROFIT ORGANIZATIONS (5th ed., Prentice Hall 1996).

NATIONAL EXECUTIVE SERVICE CORPS., STRATEGIC PLANNING FOR NONPROFIT ORGANIZATIONS (re-released Spring 1999. SHARON M. OSTER, STRATEGIC MANAGEMENT FOR NONPROFIT ORGANIZATIONS: THEORY AND CASES (Oxford University Press 1995).

Barbara E. Taylor, Richard P. Chait & Thomas P. Holland, *The New Work of the Nonprofit Board*, HARVARD BUSINESS REVIEW, Sept.-Oct. 1996, at 36.

Tax

See also Intermediate Sanctions.

Bibliography

William D. Andrews, *Personal Deductions in an Ideal Income Tax*, 86 HARV. L. REV. 309 (1972).

CHAUNCEY BELKNAP, THE FEDERAL INCOME TAX EXEMPTION OF CHARITABLE ORGANIZATIONS: ITS HISTORY AND UNDERLYING POLICY (IV Research Papers Sponsored by the Filer Commission on Private Philanthropy and Public Needs 2025, 1977).

Boris I. Bittker & George K. Raldert, *The Exemption of Nonprofit Organizations from Federal Income Taxation*, 85 YALE L.J. 299 (1976).

Victoria B. Bjorklund, James J. Fishman, & Daniel L. Kurtz, New York Nonprofit Law and Practice: With Tax Analysis (Michie 1997).

Jody Blazek, Tax Planning and Compliance for Tax Exempt Organizations (2d ed., John Wiley & Sons 1993).

John D. Colombo, *Why is Harvard Tax Exempt? (And Other Mysteries of Tax Exemption for Private Educational Institutions)*, 35 Ariz. L. Rev. 841 (Winter 1993).

Exempt Organization Tax Review (a monthly publication published by Tax Analysts and available on Lexis).

Mark A. Hall & John D. Colombo, *The Donative Theory of Charitable Tax Exemption*, 520 Ohio St. L.J. 1379 (1991).

Henry Hansmann, *The Rationale for Exempting Nonprofit Organizations from Corporate Income Taxation*, 91 Yale L.J. 54 (1981).

Frances R. Hill & Barbara L. Kirschren, Federal and State Taxation of Exempt Organizations (Warren, Gorham and Lamont 1994).

Marilyn Phelan, Nonprofit Enterprises: Law and Taxation (Callaghan, with annual loose-leaf updates, 1993).

John G. Simon, *The Tax Treatment of Nonprofit Organizations: A Review of Federal and State Policies in the Nonprofit Sector, in* 68 A Research Handbook (Walter W. Powell, ed., 1987).

U.S. Treasury Department, Internal Revenue Service, Exempt Organizations Continuing Professional Education Technical Instruction Program Textbook (Government Printing Office, prepared annually).

U.S. Treasury Department, Internal Revenue Service, Exempt Organizations Extending Professional Educators Technical Instruction Program Textbook (Government Printing Office, prepared annually).

U.S. Treasury Department, Internal Revenue Services, Tax Exempt Status for Your Organization (Publication No. 557 2001).

Case Law

Associated Master Barbers & Beauticians of America v. Commissioner, 69 T.C. 53 (1977).

Big Mama Rag v. United States, 631 F.2d 1030 (D.C. Cir. 1980).

Blake v. Commissioner, 697 F.2d 473 (2d Cir. 1982).

Bob Jones Univ. v. United States, 461 U.S. 574 (1983).
Goldsboro Art League v. Commissioner, 75 T.C. 337 (1980).
Hutchinson Baseball Enter., Inc. v. Commissioner, 696 F.2d 757 (10th Cir. 1982).
United States v. Brown Univ., 5 F.3d 658 (3d Cir. 1993).

Statutory and Other Authority

I.R.C. §§ 132, 170, 501(c), 501(h), 507, 509, 513, 1222, 3301, 4911–4912, 4940, 4941, 4942, 4943, 4944, 4945, 4946, 4958, 6104 (2002).
I.R.S. Forms 990, 990–F, 990–T, 1023, 1024, 8282, 8283.
T.D. 8920, 2001–8 I.R.B. 654.
T.D. 8308, 55 Fed. Reg. 35, 579 (Aug. 31, 1990).
Temp. Treas. Reg. § 53.4958.
Treas. Reg. § 1.107–1(a) (as amended in 1963).
Treas. Reg. §§ 1.501(c)(3)–(1)(a), (b), (c) (as amended in 1990).
Treas. Reg. § 1.501(c)(4)–1 (as amended in 1990).
Treas. Reg. §§ 1.508.1(a)(1)–1.508.1(a)(3) (as amended in 1995).
Treas. Reg. § 1.6033–2(8) (as amended in 1995).
Treas. Reg. §§ 53.4941, 53.4943, 53.4944, 53.4945, 69.545.
Rev. Rul. 67–246, 1967–2 C.B. 104.

Taxation by Municipalities

Bibliography

EVELYN BRODY, PROPERTY TAX EXEMPTION FOR CHARITIES: MAPPING THE BATTLEFIELD (2001).
William R. Ginsberg, *The Real Property Tax Exemption of Nonprofit Organizations: A Perspective,* 53 TEMP. L. REV. 291 (1980).

Technology

Internet Sites

National Strategy for Nonprofit Technology, A Blueprint for Infusing Technology into the Nonprofit Sector, April 1999, *available at* <http://www.nsnt.org>.

Trade Associations

Bibliography

JERALD A. JACOBS, ASSOCIATION LAW HANDBOOK, THIRD EDITION (American Society of Association Executives 1996).

Unrelated Business Income

Bibliography

Evelyn Brody, *A Taxing Time for the Bishop Estate: What Is the I.R.S. Role in Charity Governance?*, 21 HAWAII L. REV. 537 (1999).

Timothy L. Horner & Hugh H. Makens, *Nonprofit Symposium: Securities Regulation of Fundraising Activities of Religious and Other Nonprofit Organizations*, 27 STETSON L. REV. 473 (1997).

Faith Stevelman Kahn, *Pandora's Box: Managerial Discretion and the Problem of Corporate Philanthropy*, 44 UCLA L. REV. 579 (1997).

Case Law

Hi-Plains Hosp. v. United States, 670 F.2d 528 (5th Cir. 1982).

National Collegiate Athletic Ass'n v. Commissioner, 914 F.2d 1417 (10th Cir. 1990).

Sierra Club, Inc. v. Commissioner, 86 F.3d 1526 (9th Cir. 1996).

United States v. American College of Physicians, 475 U.S. 834 (1986).

Zeta Beta Tau Fraternity, Inc. v. Commissioner, 87 T.C. 421 (1986).

Volunteer Protection Act

Statutory and Other Authority

Volunteer Protection Act, 42 U.S.C. §§ 14501–14505 (1997).

Additional Internet Resources

Additional Internet Resources

Alliance for Nonprofit Management (devoted to improving the management and governance capacity of nonprofits), <http://www.allianceonline.org>.

American Association of Fundraising Council (promotes the need for professional and ethical standards of practice, and influences the creation of laws governing philanthropy), <http://www.aafrc.org>.

Armed Forces Insurance (an insurance company serving uniformed military professionals and their families), <http://www.afi.org>.

Association of Fundraising Professionals (formerly the National Society of Fundraising Executives; offers educational programs and programs, like the Executive Leadership Institute and Audioconference series, to improve the fund-raising profession), <http://www.afpnet.org>.

Association of Information and Image Management (AIIM) (connects users with suppliers who can help them apply document and content technologies to improve their internal processes), <http://www.aiim.org>.

Association of Records Managers and Administrators (ARMA) (publishes numerous resources for records and information management professionals), <http://www.arma.org/publications/publications.cfm>.

Association of Small Foundations, (provides information and assistance to small philanthropy foundations), <http://www.smallfoundations.org>.

Better Business Bureau (BBB) Wise Giving Alliance (formed with the merger of the National Charities Information Bureau and the Council of Better Business Bureaus Foundation and its Philanthropic Advisory Service; collects and distributes information on hundreds of nonprofit organizations that solicit nationally or have national or international program services), <http://give.org>.

California Department of Justice, Registry of Charitable Trusts, (offers information and assistance in evaluating solicitations from charities and commercial fund-raisers), <http://www.caag.state.ca.us/charities>.

The Chronicle of Philanthropy (a news source for charity leaders, fund raisers, grant makers, and other people involved in the philanthropic enterprise), <http://www.philanthropy.com>.

Corporate Governance (focuses on corporate governance topics in the for-profit area), <http://www.corpgov.net>.

Council on Foundations (helps foundation staff, trustees and board members in their day-to-day grantmaking activities), <http://www.cof.org>.

Dot Org Media (a content publishing and syndication service that offers a free e-mail newsletter, web content and special reports on selected topics such as online advocacy, fundraising, and Internet presence), <http://www.dotorgmedia.org>.

Forum of Regional Association of Grantmakers, (a national network of local leaders and organizations across the United States that support effective charitable giving), <http://www.rag.org>.

The Foundation Center (an authority on institutional philanthropy dedicated to serving grantseekers, grantmakers, researchers, policymakers, the media, and the general public), <http://www.fdncenter.org>.

Free Management Library (a free community resource, hosted by the Management Assistance Program for Nonprofits, providing leaders and managers (especially those with very limited resources) basic and practical information about business, management and organizations), <http://www.mapnp.org/library>.

Hauser Center for Nonprofit Organizations at Harvard (an interdisciplinary research center at Harvard University seeking to expand understanding and accelerate critical thinking about nonprofit organizations and civil society among scholars, practitioners, policy makers and the general public), <http://www.ksg. harvard.edu/hauser/>.

Helping.org (provides comprehensive online resources and tools to help nonprofits integrate the power of the Internet to organize, recruit, fundraise and publicize their mission and successes online), <http://www.helping.org>.

Independent Sector (a national leadership forum fostering private initiative for the public good), <http://www.independentsector.org>.

Indiana University Center on Philanthropy (contains information on philanthropy through programs on research, teaching, public service, and public affairs), <http://www.philanthropy. iupui.edu>.

The Innovation Network (a national nonprofit dedicated to building the evaluation capacity of nonprofits, so they can better serve their communities), <http://www.innonet.org>.

Institute for Not-for-Profit Management, Columbia University Business School (offers graduate programs that help students develop effective management and leadership techniques for nonprofit organizations), <http://www.gsb.columbia.edu/ execed/INM/index.html>.

Internal Revenue Service (includes tax information for individuals, businesses, charities and nonprofits, government entities and tax professionals.), <http://www.irs.ustreas.gov>.

International Center for Not-for-Profit Law (ICNL) (with other international, national, and local organizations, provides technical assistance for the creation and improvement of laws and regulatory systems that permit, encourage, and regulate the not-for-profit, nongovernmental (NGO) sector in countries around the world), <http://www.icnl.org>.

Internet Nonprofit Center (publishes the Nonprofit FAQ, a resource of information provided by partcipants in many online discussions about nonprofits and their work), <http://www. nonprofits.org>.

Jossey-Bass, Inc. (publishes a wide range of books on the nonprofit sector), <http://www.josseybass.com>.

The League of Women Voters (provides information on civic participation and current public policy issues such as election reform, campaign finance reform and health care), <http://www. lwv.org>.

Mandel Center for Nonprofit Organizations (a multidisciplinary center for education, research, and community service, also offers graduate programs for nonprofit leaders and managers), <http://www.cwru.edu/mandelcenter>.

National Association of Corporate Directors (includes efficient access to helpful information regarding its publications and seminars), <http://www.nacdonline.org>.

National Center for Social Entrepreneurs (a nonprofit consulting company), <http://www.socialentrepreneurs.org>.

National Center on Philanthropy and Law at New York University School of Law (explores a broad range of legal issues affecting the nonprofit sector and provides an integrated examination of the legal doctrines related to the activities of charitable organizations), <http://www.law.nyu.edu/ncpl>.

National Executive Service Corps. (offers a broad range of consulting and advising services on Board problems and all aspects of the operations of non-profit organization), <http://www.nesc.org/flash>.

National Network of Grantmakers (provides publications, job lists, resource links and more to funders, practitioners, and grant-seekers), <http://www.nng.org>.

Nonprofit Coordinating Committee of New York (NPCC), (a nonprofit membership corporation whose goal is the protect the nonprofit sector in New York City), <http://www.npccny.org>.

Nonprofit Resource Center (a comprehensive list of links to web sites of interest to nonprofits), <http://www.not-for-profit.org/index.html>.

One Northwest (a nonprofit organization that provides technology resources and expertise to environmental groups in the Pacific Northwest), <http://www.onenw.org>.

Summit Collaborative (a nonprofit consulting company), <http://www.summitcollaborative.com/resources.html>.

TechSoup.org (web site offering technology hardware, software, and assistance to nonprofits), <http://www.techsoup.org>.

U.S. International Grantmakers (provides information on facilitating international grantmaking), <http://www.usig.org>.

Yale Program on Nonprofit Organizations (an international center for multidisciplinary studies of philanthropy, voluntarism, and nonprofit organizations), <http://www.yale.edu/divinity/ponpo>.